WHAT DILLINGER MEANT TO ME

WHAT DILLINGER MEANT TO ME

Robert Peters

The Sea Horse Press, New York City
1983

Some of these poems have appeared in the following little magazines: *Stone Cloud, The Fault, Hanging Loose, North American Review, Poets' Almanac, Mouth of the Dragon, Word Is Out, The Berkeley Poetry Review, Blue Buildings, Wormwood Review, Abraxas, Amicus Journal,* and *Poetry L/A.*
"Night-Soil" appeared in *The Windflower Home Almanac of Poetry* (Windflower Press, 1980).
I am grateful to Ted Kooser for supplying me with the little-known information about Dillinger I use in "Radio Report." Also, I greatly appreciate the faith the Wayne State University Press and Granite Books had in my work early in my career; some of these poems, including the title poem, were published by them in *The Sow's Head and Other Poems* (Wayne State, 1968) and *Bronchial Tangle, Heart System* (Granite Books, 1975).
And final thanks to an unusual friend, George Leonard, the novelist, who suggested that I return to this Wisconsin material and write about it extensively.

Library of Congress Cataloguing in Publication Data

Peters, Robert
    What Dillinger Meant To Me

                                    82-062111

ISBN 0-933322-09-7

The Sea Horse Press, 307 West 11 St., New York, NY 10014

I don't even know what killed them.
Or him. And I do not want
to think it was the loss of the blood
of manhood. There is always more of that.
    —John Logan, "The Experiment that Failed"

Shall I make sense or shall I tell the truth?
    —Randall Jarrell, "Seele in Raum"

CONTENTS

Eagle River, Wisconsin: 1930   1

One
Father   5
My Father as House-Builder   7
Snapshots with Buck, Model-A Ford,
    and Kitchen   8
Dialogue   9
Nude Father in a Lake   10
Mother   11
Miscarriage   13
Doctor   14
Games   15
Pig-Family Game   17
Smudge-Pot   18
Potato Bugs   19
Summer Litany   20
Night-Soil   21
Rat   22
Garter Snakes   24
Crane   25
Skunks   26
The Butchering   27
The Sow's Head   30

Two
Deerskin Flowage   33
Uncles   34
Memorial Day 1933   36
Bridge Climbing   38
Car Trip   40
Hot Bread   41
Biology Lesson   42
Few of Us Feel Safe Anywhere   43
That Family   44
Cousin: Snapshot 1   45
Night Swim   46
Forest Walk   47
The Lake   48
Lucy Robinson   49
Tommy McQuaker   51
Old Carlson   52

Cousins   53
Aunt   54
Married Cousin   56
Albert   57
The Secret   59

Three
Locale   63
Personal History   64
Canoe Journey   66
The Prom   70
Rites of Passage   71
Eileen   72
Carnival Man   74
Woods   75
Daniel   76
Young Man on Sunday   77
Rev. Joseph Krubsack   78
Tableau in a Lutheran Church   79

Four
What John Dillinger Meant to Me   83
Night Visitor   85
Radio Report   86
Snow Image   87
Dillinger in Wisconsin   88
The Watch-Dogs   90
Song   91
Birthday Party   92
Cow   93
Night Accident   94
Saturday at Little Bohemia   95
Purvis   96
Waiting   97
Burning   98
The Raid   99
Everywhere, Yet Nowhere   101

Coda
Now   105
Father: As Recollection or the
Drug Decides   106
Mother   109
On Not Attending My Father's Funeral   110
Burial   113

In memory of my father and mother.

WHAT DILLINGER MEANT TO ME

EAGLE RIVER, WISCONSIN: 1930

Gangsters
came to Eagle River
but not one singer
writer or painter.

I can show you
where Dillinger sweated
at Little Bohemia

where Mayor Kelly
rubbed his belly
and shot
well bodyguarded rounds of golf

where Capone's crew
sniffed danger
adjusted their knickers
masqueraded as berrypickers
in the less ominous
air of Eagle River
when the home zoo
grew too hot

and governors
La Follette and Heil
paused awhile
patted their wallets
observed the state
of the wild blueberry crop
gathered votes
were startled to note
so few folk
in that beautiful
backwoods of
logged off, mined out
land—while Herbert Hoover
chose the Brule
for hooking trout,
saw Eagle River

1

as nothing to shout about.

And yet one could/can
flounder
up to his eyes there,
and the mind could/can
blunder
frenzied there, poems
choking the throat.

ONE

FATHER

1.
A creaking on the stairs.
A nail scratches a stovepipe.
A face, furred eyes and cheeks,
hover over.

Is it Dillinger
adorned with spruce boughs,
moss? is it a monster?

My father, by synapse,
projects dreams—
his father drowned
in prairie grass. He
orphaned, school-less
tramping after
threshing crews, carnivals,
on a trail
blocked out
led by his brother
to Wisconsin
speech and singing
guitar violin
accordion mandolin
a genius for machines
for building
and repairing them:

in his hand a pickax,
under his arm a dynamite cache.

2.
He slipped into shadow
into the enfolding woods
and returned late, with game
after I had seen him
transformed
into treebranch, into wolf,
bloodsmear on snowcrust,

ephemeral whispers
garnered from
the bloodcells of swamps,
the ventricles of trees,
the cavities of a heart,
from a flashlight cell.

MY FATHER AS HOUSE-BUILDER

Cedar poles skidded by horse
from swamp to highland, stripped
of bark, hauled to the house-site
on a knoll near the public road.

A pattern in the sand
for the two rooms and kitchen, drawn
with a sapling and a rule.
Cedar poles adzed flat for the frame.
Other poles notched for walls.

We chinked logs with swamp-moss,
gathered by pails-full, held in
by slats, then plastered over.
We puttied the windows, tiny
to hold in the heat.

Scrap-lumber for the roof and floor.
A cellar hole in the livingroom,
the sand fetched up by buckets on a rope
and dumped outside in a marsh-hole
filled in for a garden plot.

The upper story, hip-roofed, low,
bedroom space for the kids,
built without plumb lines, as a
hedgehog might, in haste, hurrying
before summer blazed off
into snow and ice. Tin smoke-pipe
leaning north, tied by guy wires
to eyelets in the roof.

We nagged dad to finish the walls
with boards, which he never did.
The bare studs, he said, were good
for hanging pots, clothes, and pictures
from. The ceilings and bedroom walls
we insulated with flattened boxes
and pictures cut from the Sunday news.

SNAPSHOTS WITH BUCK, MODEL-A FORD, AND KITCHEN

1.
The buck's neck in a twist beside the car's head lamp.
His tongue sticky, pimpled cardboard.
Gashed throat. Eye glassed over. Opaque milk.
Belly slit, incision swept with blood-hair.
His hooves secured with a rope. Magnificent
twelve-pronged antlers.

2.
Dad whetted a knife on his emery stone.
A galvanized tub caught the dribbles.
He sliced off the lovely head, disjointing the neck bone.

He severed the hooves with a saw
and placed them, on paper, in a row
under the pot-bellied stove. He shucked the hide,
wet ivory integument and muscle,
would later treat it with lye
and cure it for mittens.

Grease in the black pan on the stove sizzled.
Dad pushed his thumbs into the savory venison,
Discs of marrow-bone, piles for soup.
Piles of purple meat for grinding.

We buried the venison in snow
on the roof, to be eaten as needed.
Morning, tracks circled our house.
Wolves had snapped at one another's heels all night
maddened by blood and spoor.

DIALOGUE

"You stole the dynamite, dad."

"On $40 per month, son, the WPA
won't miss it. When I build the basement
it'll be handy."

"That's robbing. . . ."

"We're poor. We've got our own laws."

"I'm scared when you go hunting."

"Don't worry, son. Just keep your nose
clean and your britches pulled up.
We've got our ways. There's struggle.
We have to make it, what ways we can."

NUDE FATHER IN A LAKE

I've never stopped, even in my sleep,
seeing him in the lake
facing me with his hands all wax
over his sex.   His throat
and his wrists are burned.
He is so white.
He splashes me with water.

I yank my baggy swim trunks off,
dive, and reach cold mud.
I hold a submerged branch.
His nudity no longer shimmers . . .
a dance . . . a fish . . . green cartilage
between his eyes . . . a hinged mouth.

I surface and watch dad
retrieve his clothes from a bush.
He keeps on walking, without asking
me, entices me to follow, from the rear.

MOTHER

Girl, sixteen,
straining over a washtub
in an iceshed of a house
chinked with moss
veiled with tarpaper

House alive with mice
in warm weather,
in cold with ice.

Your stuttering washlines
strung up
through the house:
slab underwear (flat
salted fillets) sheets,
shirts, board-stiff
dresses, nightshirts.

And the meals: pancakes
whipped out of batter
kept in a crock
fermenting on the back
of the woodstove.

Peanut butter (County Relief)
extended by blendings
of bacon drippings . . .

Repeat those gestures!
Strip away all subsequent
events! Goad us out
to the pasture, to the starved
potato field, and the bean field
while you prod, curse
your life, as night
(a peddler) drops
poisoned seed, and a
wreathing fog settles in,
soft underbelly, soft thighs,

tight against the throat
dark lovely throat
of night. I crouch again
waiting, hoping you are near.
Touch me! Touch me!

MISCARRIAGE

My mother bathes alone—
the metal tub, the kettle
of hot water, on a strip
of carpet, in her room.

She has lost another child.
Dad buries it under the birches
behind the well.

God is on her side.
She didn't want the child.
He listened to her when she cried.
He opened a fresh wound wide
in His eternal side.
The baby slipped in and hid there
when he died.

DOCTOR

He was drunk, and his breath stunk.
He wore a brown wool suit and a tan coat.
His voice was brusque demanding water,
cloths and a small brush.
His hands fluttered when he said
the birth looked bad.
The cord strangled the baby's throat.
He failed to cry.
He would die.

I saw the red body in the air.
It had black hair.

The Doctor waved us off—
"Wait in the kitchen," he said.
"We'll clean up now. The boy's fine.
We'll be done in no time."

We sat across the table.
The kerosene lamp in the middle.
My sister was staring at her knuckles.
I saw her skinny breasts, her brown hair braid,
her small, firm lips.
She looked at me. I thought she would cry.
I didn't know why.

GAMES

1.
My sister had a tiny room under the eaves
where she pretended we were hidden in willow leaves.

A moose chomped pickerel grass and yellow water lilies.
We inched forward on our bellies.

2.
We played *family*—she was always the mother.
I wanted the kids. I was tired of being the father.

"You can drive to work," she said, "and bring home flour and bacon.
I'll cook the meals, milk, and toss down the fodder.
Too bad, the mother's taken."

3.
I played her way, afraid she might not play at all.
She said "no" when I suggested *gnome* or *troll* or *ball*.

We'd quarrel. She vowed she'd run to the lake and drown herself.
I saw her gingham dress flash down the path, as death.

4.
I slept in a strawberry patch.. I hoed some corn.
I pumped cold draughts of water from the well, caught the forlorn

Clang and tinkle of cattle bells. The lake was calm.
Footprints by the shore. No cloth-scraps to show that she had gone

Into the deep, chill, ochre-tinted water. Minnows flashed
around an old boat pier. I dashed towards home.

Halfway to the pasture gate I reached an old hayrick.
My sister's sudden laughter made me sick.

5.
I flung her to the sand.
She yelled that I had sprained her hand.

I knew she'd tell our dad.
I hid until they'd gone to bed.

I crept upstairs, lay down
and drew a blanket over my head.

PIG-FAMILY GAME

I was the sow, she was the boar.
Six kitchen chairs for a pen.
We put on winter coats and grunted.
I lay on my side, coat open
and birthed six pigs.
Only one was runted. Six squirts,
minimal pain, minimal swelling.
I peeled the after-births,
then nudged the piglets into standing.
Boar was in a corner plowing up edible roots.
Sow ate the placentas.
The piglets yanked and nuzzled her teats.
Sow-milk ran, her ovaries tingled.
There was froth on her mouth,
in the black juicy loam of the pen.

SMUDGE-POT

1.
Mosquitoes
plague the house at dusk.

They bite your arms
and face at will,

plump with blood, like
small overloaded tubers.

They float to the nearest twig.
The welts burn and tingle.

2.
I cram dead leaves, paper
and shavings in a pail.

I raise the bail, strike the fire,
then douse it with wet grass.

Smoke-roilings! I bathe and drench
the house. I shut the screens tight
and hope I'll sleep that night.

POTATO BUGS

Dad paid us a nickel a quart to pick the bugs.
The plants, just blossoming, were infested.
By dropping the bugs into a jar, fast,
they didn't juice our fingers.
They exuded a noisome odor.
We poured in kerosene.

When dad paid us
we drained the fluid to use again,
dumped the dead bugs on the manure-pile
behind the barn.

SUMMER LITANY

"If we don't pick berries
we'll starve this winter," mom said.
Dad was sweat-soaked from working
in the field. "We'll paint our butts
with varnish to keep 'em warm
if some money don't come in."

"Rob the bank, pa."

"Those rich buggers, floating on top,
ought to spread their money around."

Dad knocked his pipe against the stove,
stood up, stretched, and yawned.

"Maybe that Dillinger or whoever's
robbin' the banks will come out here
and help us."

NIGHT-SOIL

It was always this way:
    each spring dad shovelled up
       outhouse winter deposits.

He dug into the pile from the rear,
    shovelled it onto a stone-boat
       hauled it to the fields,
    borrowing my uncle's horse.

Pages torn from Sears catalogues
    stuck to the soil, patchwork of
       men and boys in underwear
    cheap suits, overalls, tough boots and shoes.

Dad claimed he knew each Saturday's deposit,
    when we ate peanuts, played cards,
       and heard the *Hit Parade*.

He strewed the offal over the fields,
    then plowed it under. The disk
       restored some to the surface

Where squash and corn grew large and green
    sprouting from night-soil,
       rich, rich ordure, human.

RAT

1.
We heard him in the cellar-pit
below the floor. Dad lifted the door,
shot down a light, caught him
in a beam, on a pile of sand.
Milky potato roots writhed
up the stone walls. I saw
the yellow teeth.

2.
Dad built a trap from an apple-crate.
We smoked the box to smear out human smell.
Inside we threw some wheat. A rigged door.
We waited to hear the trap latch,
for the rat to screech and scramble.
At midnight we went to bed.

3.
Next morning dad left for work
on the WPA crew. Nothing new
in the cellar. "He's too smart,"
dad said, "We'll have to shoot him."

4.
I was stoking the wood-stove fire . . .
an incredible bang and rattle!
Mom rushed in from the kitchen.
"We've caught him!" I shouted.

5.
I raised the trap.
The rat plunged and snarled.
He gnawed the wood. He bit through
the chicken-wire.

We removed the stove's top lid
and slid the trap, door down over
the flames. I opened the trap.
The rat clung to the screen.

22

We beat his toes with a poker.
I struck his teeth.
He fell into the fire.

GARTER SNAKES

There was so little to do.
We caught big garter snakes
And hacked them in two.

They slithered best when the days were blue.
We found them in the pasture and
Near the outhouse where mullein grew.

We knew they ate mice and rats.
We believed they devoured cats.
They were vicious, satanic—we thought we knew.

They hissed and tried to bite us—
What else would a snake do?
They jiggled long after they were cut in two.

(I noticed drops of snakeblood on my shoe.)
We draped the chunks over a barbed-wire fence,
Sure that we'd saved our innocence.

We joked, saying snake would make good stew.
That's what Indians were supposed to do—
Brew up snake, rat, stoat, and caribou.

Around the farm our fears and superstitions blew.
We thought we knew. We thought we knew.

CRANE

A gray crane on a rock glares.
He might be stuffed,
except that an eye blinks.
He scrapes his beak
on his wing, raises a leg.
I grab a stone.
A bone cracks.
A red eye swims.
Feathers fly in the wind.

SKUNKS

1.

A skunk stomps his feet,
erects his tail, tip down,
and then by raising the tip
spins noisome fluid from his anal
glands up over you.
The odor spreads for half a mile.

2.

They are frequently smashed by cars.
Instead of running, they hold ground.

3.

They burrowed under our coop.
One scooped dirt, hid in a gasoline tank
dad had converted to a heater. The skunk
nipped off several hens, sucked
their blood, stuffed the tank
with their bodies.

4.

Dad fished the animal out with a pitch-fork
and buried it. We stripped
the dead hens. My mother canned the meat.
It tasted sweet.

THE BUTCHERING

1.
Dad told me to hold the knife
and the pan. I heard the click
on wood of the bullet inserted,
rammed. Saw a flicker thrash
in a tree beside the trough,
saw a grain in the sow's mouth,
felt my guts slosh.

"Stand back," dad said.
Waffled snow track
pressed by his boots and mine.
Blood and foam. "Keep the knife
sharp, son, and hold the pan."
One of us had shuffled,
tramped a design,
feet near the jackpine.
"She'll bleed slow.
Catch all the blood you can."

A rose unfolded, froze.
"Can't we wait?" I said.
"It should turn warmer."

Spark, spark buzzing
in the dark.

"It's time," dad said, and waited.

2.
Bless all this beauty! preacher
had exclaimed; *all sin and beauty
in this world! Beast and innocent!*

Fistbones gripped the foreshortened
pulpit rim. Thick glasses drove
his furious pupils in.

3.
Dad brought the rifle to the skull.
The sow's nose plunged into the swill,
the tips of her white tallow ears as well.
Splunk! Straight through the brain, suet
and shell. Stunned! Discharge of food,
bran. Twitch of an ear. Potato, carrot,
turnip slab. "Quick. The knife, the pan."

He sliced the throat.
The eye closed over.
Hairy ears stood up, collapsed.
Her blood soured into gelatin.
She had begun to shit.

4.
We dragged her
to the block and tackle rig.
We tied her tendons, raised her,
sloshed her up and down.
We shaved her hair,
spun her around, cut off
her feet and knuckles,
hacked off her head,
slashed her belly
from asshole down through
bleached fat throat.
Jewels spilled out
crotches of arteries
fluids danced and ran.

We hoisted her
out of dog reach
dumped her entrails
in the snow
left the head
for the dogs to eat—
my mother disliked head-meat.
The liver, steaming monochrome,
quivered with eyes.
We took it home.

5.
I went to my room.
Tongues licked my neck.
I spread my arms,
threw back my head.
The tendons of a heel
snapped.
What had I lost?
bit   bridle   rage?

Preacher in his pulpit
fiddling, vestments aflame.
He, blazing, stepping down
to me. Hot piss came.
I knelt on the floor,
bent over, head in arms.
Piss washed down, more.
I clasped my loins,
arm crossed over arm.
And I cried
loving my guts,
O vulnerable guts,
guts of creatures.

THE SOW'S HEAD

The day was like pewter.
The gray lake a coat
open at the throat. The border
of trees—frayed mantle collar,
hairs, evergreen. The sky dun.
Chilling breeze. Hem of winter.

I passed the iodine-colored brook
hard waters open
the weight of the sow's head
an ache from shoulder to waist,
the crook of my elbow numb.
Juices seeping through
the wrapping paper.

I was wrong to take it.
There were meals in it.
I would, dad said, assist
with slaughter, scrape off
hair, gather blood.
I would be whipped for
thieving from the dogs.

I crossed ice
which shivered, shone.
No heads below, none;
nor groans—only water, deep,
and the mud beds of frogs asleep;
not a bush quivered,
not a stone. Snow.

Old snow had formed
hard swirls   bone
and planes with
windwhipped ridges
for walking upon;
and beneath, in the deep,
bass quiet, perch whirling
fins, bluegills, sunfish,

dim-eyed soaking heat.
Mud would be soft down there,
rich, tan, deeper than a man:
silt of leeches, leaves
tumbling in from trees,
loon feces, mulch-thick
mudquick, and lignite forming,
cells rumbling, rifts.

I knelt, chopped through
layers of ice until
water, pus, spilled up
choking the wound. I widened
the gash. Tchick! Tchick!
Chips of ice flew.
Water blew from the hole,
the well, a whale, expired.
My knees were stuck to the ice.

I unwrapped the paper.
The head appeared
shorn of its beard.
Its ears stood up, the snout
with its Tinker Toy holes
held blood. Its eyes were shut.
There was grain on its mouth.

It sat on the snow
as though it lived below,
leviathan come for air
limbs and hulk
dumb to my presence there.

I raised the sow's head
by its ears. I held it
over the hole, let it go,
watched it sink, a glimmer
of pink, a wink of a match
an eyelid . . .

A bone in my side beat.

TWO

DEERSKIN FLOWAGE

The river is mineral-red.
A trout snaps at a may-fly.

You can't see where the bones lie,
Glacial, among boulders.

UNCLES

1.

My uncles were gassed in the trenches,
pissed out their fear in the trenches

saw horses blown to scrap,
dragged comrades from barbedwire traps
fought off bronze rats
in Ypres, Belleau Wood,
Chateau-Thierrey, Verdun.

2.

Don't be afraid, son,
if there's war you'll come back.

And when you're forty, home,
you'll rest in a swamp of death,
dying all around.

I'll die then, and you won't know.
It's dirty. No wishing on a moon, son,
wow!

3.

Trailing piss
my uncles run
       nowhere
to place hands
       nowhere
to insert wound-rags
       nowhere
to scream, blare
claw smoke
       nowhere
to latch the mask
no nose to
hang it from
throat, lingam
shot away, shapes
dangle from bones

running, running this way,
running.

MEMORIAL DAY 1933

1.
Observe
how no ornament impedes
your climb.

The girders are red-orange
triangles and lines.
Pillars beneath

north and south
connect the dim side of town
with the other side.

2.
Hang by an upper girder.
Swing out
over Eagle River.

The sun is white.
The dentist is in his
aeroplane.

3.
Zoom. Zoom.
A rapt crowd.
Dr. MacIntyre's
aviator cap.

The quiet motor.
The slap of an arm.

A wreath of poppies
hits the river . . .
In Flanders Field.

4.
Rifle shots.
The cannonade.
More fusilades.

The two-winged plane
dips low in homage
and speeds away.

Flag-colors at noon.
Milton Boho's silver whistle:
the high school band
starts its march to the cemetery.

BRIDGE CLIMBING

That still point
that point
beyond the girders,
the steeple,
that still point
in the eyes of those
who've felt
they're anointed
peeling the last orange
peeling off their clothes
their eyes peeled
their intercostal muscles,
heart-fibers, nerves.

that still point

poised on the girders
among swallows
I balance
this morning, sunday
wanting . . .

Like a cat about its business
I have buried disturbing questions.

And yet
there are flames,
burnings, scribblings
by some unkempt hand
in a language
I can't read
of a tongue
I can't understand.

I think it has to do
with sex, anxiety
or the rope of the self
drawn tight
about the throat

about the groin

that still point

Up on the girders
swaying above
the curved town,
my arms out
from my body—
I know my weight
and my height.
The curve of the river
is a perimeter,
the undulating clouds
form another.
I won't come down.

CAR TRIP

This sandy-haired uncle
was twenty. I was five.
I remember his hand
as he drew me up
beside him in his car.
We left Wisconsin at night,
in his model-A ford,
going to North Dakota
to visit my grandmother,
near Fargo.
As he drove, I put my head
in his lap. He stroked my face.
Heat rose from the floorboards.
The motor purred.
When he stopped, he changed
my clothes and bathed me
and put me to bed, where
I snuggled against him,
and fell asleep.

HOT BREAD

Over and over again, from the start,
he stands on the rim of the gravel-pit
staring at Clark Gable, shirtless, wearing
dark glasses, near a whitepine.

When he comes, the hole he feels in his heart
hurts as much as it did before:
he can't go west! He can't study law!
He can't teach or sing. . . .

He smells fresh bread, and he wipes
himself with leaves. In the kitchen
as he eats he knows that a half is enough,
the raisin, or the unmilled wheat,
in the hot, sweet loaf.

BIOLOGY LESSON

A spotted newt
beneath a pile of leaves.
Three more beneath a stone.
They're quick—you slap your hand
and catch them to take home.
You put them in a jar.
You take them to school.
They hibernate far down
in the muck and leaves.

They drown, or so it seems.
You find them: limp, white bits
of pork fuzzed with mold.
Was the jar too cold?
the sugar-water too sweet?
You throw them out.
Instead, you hatch frog-eggs
from a pond, find turtles buried in hot sand
near a log, catch twenty
still-blind field mice.

FEW OF US FEEL SAFE ANYWHERE

He recalls
digging up moleroutes,
looking for moles,
in a schoolyard.
The mangy grass
bound and flattened by
mud and water rose up
beneath soft channels
burrowed by molesnouts.

He unearthed
a fertile nest, fought
down two friends to keep
the blind pink furless
creatures to himself,
warm between his hands.

He won by
running up to teacher
intending to present her
with those jewels, his catch
a quest, possession all
his own, for her, his lover.

But others
watched, grinned
as he drew apart those palms,
revealed those pinkish forms,
stilled, calm, their shanks
of legs drawn up beneath
their toothless jaws, their
whiskers bent, their mouths
each bearing blood.

THAT FAMILY

That family had ten kids. They bred like rabbits.

That family used their fingers to eat from pots
of venison and beans.

That family tapped maple trees for sap, fished and hunted—
they sniffed animal spoor, like beagles.

That family never wiped their asses clean—there was no paper.

That family slept four to a bed, the girls slept with their parents.

That family tied up the oldest brother's morning erection,
hooked the string to the ceiling, woke him with a yank,
induced an ejaculation.

That family—the mother had great brown breasts and a hairy chin.
She wore one single dirty dress fastened with safety pins.

That family played hot pinochle, poker and rummy.
They never went to church or believed in the Easter Bunny.

That family worked at the sawmill in town, swilled booze,
had fist-fights and spent nights in jail.

That family took me fishing, taught me sex in the barn, and invited
me swimming. We showed our asses to the girls and called them
"moons." I loved that family. They were fantasy country,
somewhere south of Eden, north of Daniel's den.

COUSIN: SNAPSHOT 1

I see him
nude on a tamarack log
poised over Minnow Lake
ready to plunge.
He doesn't see me.
His throat is tan, as are
his hands.
His body ripples.

He's making hand motions.
I want to stroke him.
I want the timing right.
We jerk with the same thrust:
cream flies away on the stream.
This is neither fantasy nor dream.

NIGHT SWIM

The wild apples were bitter, as we knew
they were. We skipped them
over the lake, quit finally and built
a fire on the shore. Three of us
crouched near the flames.
Toads swam to the firelight
from all over the lake.
On the oily surface, their knobby heads
left wakes. I reached along the sand
and touched Bill's scrotum.
I held him in my hand, as the toads hopped
from the black water, croaking,
tumbling over one another
in foul copulation, beside the fire.

FOREST WALK

Cedar, spruce, and pine.
Jack-rabbit tracks, red snow,
Offal pellets, yellow rounds of urine.

            Where's the lake?

Deer trails moving south.
Buck and doe. Rush of snow
Tumbling from spruce trees.

            Snow is a smoke, powdering the trail.

Fox yip, partridge clatter, bubbling
Stream. Rifle shot. Moss-ice
Red spoor encased in blue.

            Let's start back.

Rotten pine stump, freshly clawed
By a bear. Nest of piss-ants,
A prize. We eat them, peppered slivers of ice.

            A sheltering pine. The snow thickens.

Brittle pickerel-weed and flag on a glazed stream.
Click of rubber boots, cracking ice, lake-thunder
Startled geese.
            I knew! The sun broke through.

THE LAKE

The lake is anvil-shaped,
its edges roughened, off-center,
as the boys said it was,
the boys who fished there
each summer, who boasted later
boys from town
with their own canoes
bought, not built like mine,
pretested on the water.

In the mind:
crippled trees—a brainful.
The lake is a shape, in a haze,
a rasping wind. Shore foliage
and water weeds.

No one will find you here.

LUCY ROBINSON

Lucy Robinson's
rimless spectacles
rode athwart her nose.
About her neck
were chunks of fur
which made it appear
that she had tiny rabbits on.
Masses of hair
hung down her face
(old curtains belted low
about the waist). Her
wrists were fat. Her
hands were knobs, the
knuckles bumps and knots
which creaked to open.
Her mouth seldom parted
when she spoke.

Through the musty curtains
she would come
shattering the sleep
of moths, hums of flies,
raising dust.

Massive creature
keeping the shoestore
in the parlor
of her decayed lath house,
selling one pair a day,
two before school began
and more for Santa Claus.

I see her with a box
fetched from a shelf
behind a cage. Dad
pulls me up, points
to a brightening shoe.

Lucy wheezes and the light

is dim. Her arthritic
finger latches in
behind my heel. A dead bird.
I feel its bill.

I want her hand free!
the size to be right!
The shoes will pinch and blister.
I shall have to break them in evenings
drawing water for the cows!

She stuffs dollars
in the tight mouse
of her hand, whiskers
on her knuckles twitch,
and whiskers on her mouth . . .

In that debris,
in the dust
a hunger now—except for
an image, a lampwink,
a jewel, a gland
(faint radium pulse)
a spotted lung, striations
on a hand, an arthritic spur,
a claw quivering near a baseboard
hole . . . What have you done
Lucy Robinson?

TOMMY McQUAKER

Tommy McQuaker's soft fat dad
clerked at the bank.
His bosomy mother Pearl
talked a lot. Her orange hair
was tightly curled.

Tommy was home only in summer.
He walked like a woman down Main
Street, and led a poodle on a leash
and smiled. He wore shorts, sandals,
and a polkadot tie.

We said he lacked balls
that he cupped his hands
around his cock when he peed.
He was into theater and poetry.
He had a "boyfriend" in Chicago.
That town's exotic.

I'd walk three miles to see him
strut his dog, greeting
his mother's friends.

I kept my distance, as I did
from Catholic nuns, on the far side
of the street.

I feared Tommy'd bite my lips
and give me diseases. I craved
his obscene squeezes.

OLD CARLSON

Evergreens were buried to their tops.
There were no tracks in the snow.
I decided to visit old Carlson,
living alone forty acres away, in the storm.
Sunset, iridescent sky-breath,
sun-dogs purplish cold, red-gold
slashed clouds.

Snow swirled about his house
like a hot tongue, leaving the earth
bare. Drifts sluiced. My rubber boots
kept me warm. Drops of breath froze
on my scarfs and mittens.

I knocked. A shuffle. A cough.
A hen danced over a wooden floor.
Snow blew from the roof.

"Come in," he said. Coal-oil stench.
His gray underwear was unbuttoned
at the waist. Greenish pubic hair.
Testicles and old penis dangling there.

"Have some coffee, come eat a bite."

"I have to do the chores," I said.

Spun-sugar breath followed me home.
The man's penis cascaded foam.
My testes shrivelled into tiny stones.

COUSINS

They slept three to a bed.
Winter and summer they wore
split-seat underwear.
They were in their teens.
I was twelve.

A late-spring storm. Severe.
My aunt says, "Stay the night,
with the boys, in the big bed."

I undress in the dark, fear they'll see
my pubic hairs and my tiny cock.
They doff their clothes in a heap
and are ready to sleep:
Albert on the outside,
French in the middle, then Jim.
"Jump in."

I lie on my back.
Aromatic breaths. Fear. I turn.
French's rear is bare. Albert
snuggles. My heel touches
his balls. I pretend to sleep.
His penis hardens. It snakes
my buttocks, and I wait.
My craving funnels itself,
roilings of sweat, sweet stench
of ivory and leek.

AUNT

The river drowned its banks,
washed down fields, nests,
stray planks, cats, dogs, porcupines.
It reached her farm
sloshed through her barns and sheds,
encircled the log house on its mound,
dropped towards the lake,
fetching in its wake
three occasions (two of which I saw)
universals in this conundrum—
the if and when:

a:
Her eldest son
dead by the garage.
A bullet in his head
his leg drawn up
stiffening.

b:
A fire smothered the summer.
Crews imported trucks, shovels
to fight the blaze.
Her farm was a base.

c:
With mower rope she
tied herself to a joist
ripped her dress
from neck to hem
took advantage
of her menstrual flow
screamed to the god
of virgins she
was ravished, found
her victim in an aging man
who resisted her
advances, and who
went to prison, despite

his protestations
languished there
and died.

d:
I found her in bed
the covers thrown back
a hole the size
of a fish's sphincter
ripped
below her navel.
A trace of powder
a folded rose of pain
rubbed smut against her.

He did it, she screamed.
The son of a bitch!
After all these years.

We found her revolver
under the woodpile
where she had thrown it.
We found it the next
afternoon.

MARRIED COUSIN

To stand near Matt
was to be in detention, bound
by one of Matt's guitar strings.
He tried being nonchalant, smooth.
But he tripped and fell
into a jangle of strings.

He slept with Matt when Matt's wife
was having a baby. Matt's groin
smelled of swamp and onions.

"I want to run off with you," he said,
behind barbed wire, before Matt
drifted to sleep. "We'll hunt
deer, and fish out of season. . . ."
He craved to kiss Matt, to break his bones!

"You're too young," Matt said.
"Well, I'm already nine. I'll love
you even more. . . ." "Go to sleep, Bobby."

He chewed bitter clover. His thighs ached
as men, cut from wrapping paper,
with brimmed hats and holsters, guns drawn,
surrounded him, and yanked off his breech-cloth.

Another unsprung trap.

ALBERT

He was as hated a a runted shoat.
He was his mother's not his dad's. He wore no colored coat.
They beat him with horse-harness, as they would.
They called him bastard, and told him to be good.

He had to do chores, as the younger brother said,
And hoe the corn and chop the wood.
Whenever he went alone to the lake for swimming,
They waited to give him another trimming.

He smiled at strangers, excelled at school,
Was liked by the teachers.
He was lithe and tall, with jet-black eyes and hair.
The girls stared and giggled.

He clerked hard in a grocery store one summer.
His folks took half his money for room and board.
He bought an old Model-T, gabardine pants, a shirt and tie,
A 21-rifle, and a strong light to check his beaver traps by.

That winter he shot two bucks for food,
And caught the largest pike, fishing through the ice.
He chopped half the winter's supply of wood.
When they killed the sow he caught the blood.

Spring came. A row over the plowing.
He was needed at the store and begged off farming.
His half-brother Jim chased him with an axe, and
Screamed he would kill him.

His leg was hacked. The bone-pain shimmered.
He grappled with his brother.
His mother struck him with the axe-haft.
It splintered in pieces over his back.

He gasped, freed himself, and ran through the trees
Beyond the meadow. He swam in the icy lake
Out past the middle, dove, retrieved handfuls of loam
And when he was spent, returned home.

He strode past the men who were plowing.
He entered the house, ignoring his mother's shouts.
He grabbed his rifle, inserted a shell
Announced he would shoot himself, down by the well.

"You won't!" his mother screamed and barred the door.
He shoved her aside and cocked the gun.
He knew she was watching through the window glass.
He bled to death in the deep green grass.

THE SECRET

He knew he would be a man.
It had to be God's plan.
He was adept at chopping wood,
Milking cows, looked after the hen's brood.
He talked dirty with boys at school,
Cultivated an interest in his dad's farm tools,
Imagined the family he would someday sire,
Tried business by selling garden seeds and picture-frame
wire. He fondled girls' breasts in his dreams,
Expressed his guilt in night-screams,
Watched his cousin Grace at the lake disrobe,
Went along with the local homophobes.

THREE

LOCALE

Locale is a symbol
is a violet
which near path or walk
trembles as it unfolds.

It can be photographed
and mapped
can be limned with chalk
and can be painted.

But
as lodestone or magnet
a violet
can be transfixed
if at all

by wailing
(honey or gall)
by a mouth
spewing shapes:
the gasping O

trying to recall
figures seen
as in a scrim
as in a dream
and that is all.

PERSONAL HISTORY

1.
At twelve
I had myself baptized
induced my family to attend church
taught sunday school
mowed down various
adolescent heresies
with the jawbone of my
zeal, sang Solomon's songs
and erotic hymns,
savored the cannibalism
of wafer and wine, made
the savior's wounds my own,
displayed myself upon crosses,
prayed myself into onanistic
sweats during pounding
thunderstorms, dressed in a
sheet, communed with my
lover, saw the world
entirely as glass.

2.
To walk three miles
on a Sunday, a hick boy
strewn with the ids
of his ancestors.

To see his first movie
Rose Marie I love You.

Warbling away
those singers smothered
mountains with
layers of chocolate sound.

But my mother's hats
were not Jeanette's.
And I never saw my dad,
strawboss of a WPA

crew lead his troop of men,
shovels over shoulder
sing out his lungs
in a hairy-chested
marching song.

CANOE JOURNEY

1.
The canoe
slides easily down
from the top
of the model-A Ford.

I launch it
regard the trees
shivering aspen
huddling wall.

Is there blood?

I see headlamp eyes,
saliva, and a
hairy jaw . . .
My dad's tracks race
through the woods.

2.
My knees touch
the metal mouldridge
of the sides.
Cordstrand of trousers.

A bursting river
swollen now
where water
newly freed from ice
is glazed
by an oleaginous dark . . .

If I could reach bottom
and rend that cluster
of underwater garnets
broken on granite!

3.
I pass demolished trees

where a storm
has splattered them.
Debris is kindling-spun.

I slide beneath
tamarack and spruce.

The dipping of a spoon
into a springful of water.

Grabbing branches
I slide the boat along
pass through
a bronchial tangle, heart
system.

The air is sweet
with alcohol and blood,
no houses near, no farms,
deserted.

I skim through
and come to a meadow
faint frozen green,
red moss-spoor,
the sky smoky,
anger in the clouds,
blue, a dram of it, and red.
The blue vanishes.
The sun is faint,
suddenly hurricanic.

I beach the canoe.
Birds rise.
The canoe wavers
at sapling anchor
strains for midstream
and lake, muskellunge
in cold waterbrake.

Beneath the marshgrass
routes for ferrets

tracks for snouts, mouths
feeding on veins,
capillary streams.

My boots are soaked
past the laces.

I am in past my knees.

4.
Whish and *slash* of weedspear,
scrape and tear of lilypad,
scum on spruce branches.

The prow rises.
The paddle drips fine silt.

Air, sharp diamond,
pricks my throat.
My shirt is soaked.
Pikeweed
trails from my hand.

A mouth, gelatin hard
swirls and sinks.
A muskellunge strikes.
Water and a stone
mica-shining below . . .

I crave for a voice, for
a hunter (my father), for
a soldier, for a swimmer,
for my dead cousin
for Dillinger.

5.
The sun blisters forth,
a tangle within a body, within
a chest, as the canoe fans,
turns upon a vitrescent wave
the color of cinnamon.

The north sky slides
with icelight in daylight.
A wind clatters reeds and grasses
drenched with ice.

A merganser honks, banks and
drops a shadow,
strikes north, disappears.
A claw draws up a black lamp
towards Cassiopeia.

THE PROM

I asked her to the dance
then ran
from school, from home,
from my ugly clothes.

I gave her flowers:
a gardenia, an orchid, a pink
tea rose. I pinned them clumsily
to her clothes.

She would not dance with me.
She danced with many others.
I apologized for being green.
She wouldn't be seen, she said,
stumbling and fumbling.

I left her in a field of crows.
I ran five miles home,
five miles to my bed,
five miles to the quilt over my head.

RITES OF PASSAGE

1.
Snow patches.
Stone-marrow, maidenhair
Faint rubbery buds, at dusk.
Star-flower moss.
Mist-swallowing water steaming,
welling from
whirling and ashes,
subterranean
limpid and potent, sexual flow
and current.

2.
Coyotes yipped and howled.
Fir trees cracked with cold.
Moonlight flashed snow.
A stream spewed ice, gurgled
and flowed. Blue-ice stars
swung within reach. A teal cloud
covered the moon.
Vertical tiers of magnificent
northern lights!

EILEEN

1.
Meet me
in the dark
root cellar

earth, a kerosene
light, burlap,
no thought of morning

to answer this
why without
flowers you

overwhelm me
with orchids
and violets

to the act of
my loving you
myself as
rigid earth in
the darkness
lying

without blankets
for hours
in the musk

without caring
brought into it
into its particular

treasure, the
pounding hooves
of goats, the
red tongues
of parrots.

2.
It was a mood
disrupting
the black fog
throwing off
singly
the burlap bags.

Who could be
natural?

the pickle jars
sneering overhead
the stench
of rotting potatoes
whiffed sensuality
fat wet mushrooms,
carrots, onions
softening.

Nor did
fantasy work.
Erect it shrivelled
when you said
"Don't be dirty."

I dropped free
dressed again
in the black house
of my own clothing
but did not know it.

CARNIVAL MAN

I tried to lock the door.
The sound of whipped leaves was hard to bear.
I pounded my feet on the floor.
I should not have gone to the fair.

I had helped him erect the tent.
We both held the central pole.
He was southern, brown, magnificent.
I was his branch, he was my bole.

I watched him undress in his trailer.
He thought I was older then.
He gave me two dollars for my labor,
and said "keep growing"—he'd be back again.

I couldn't lock the door.
Horses were loose in the storm.
I huddled on the floor.
I shouldn't have gone to the fair!

WOODS

A meadow in the pines and birches.
Wild-clover, strawberry vines
and larches. Timothy-heads, plantain,
Indian pipe, hawkweed, wild gentians.
The stones in the path absorbed my heat.
Sunlight. I removed my overalls, undressed.

A clutch of sperm induced, directed, spent,
is a precious element:
hot translucent pearly testament
zinc, iron, copper, and aluminum.

DANIEL

From his upstairs bedroom window he sees violets. It's winter.
He thinks it's amusing, the bang and tingle of fire swelling the
stove-pipe. Creosote smell. Six inches from his face anemones
of frost, nipples around nail-ends poking through the roof. He
laughs, catching water on his tongue. He grabs the Bible, opens it
to the mezzotint of Daniel facing the beasts. Daniel's cheek is
downy. His lips are as sweet as hawthorn berries. His throat
is musky. His belly is arbutus and fresh milk.

YOUNG MAN ON SUNDAY

The mirror reflects his teeth.
He plasters his hair with brilliantine.

He walks two miles to Sunday school.
He memorizes one psalm walking in, one walking home.

He rehearses the Golden Rule.
His pupils are town kids, Lutherans.

He exhorts them to Jesus. Fear is love.
Love is fear. Pennies dropping.

REV. JOSEPH KRUBSACK

He always glowered from the pulpit,
for we had broken all ten commandments
simply by being born. Behind the reredos
a fox chewed his entrails.
Pain rounded his vowels.
He sputtered Teutonic hisses.
To his right, above the altar, Jesus
wearing his pastel robes and a touch
of red on a nipple
extended a beneficent lean arm.

Slowly Rev. Krubsack embalmed himself.
The winds of sin smacked his jowls.
His chinfolds turned to icy tallow.
He crushed a silver communion cup
between his teeth and swallowed it.

Frightened, I saw the blood on my
county welfare suit, and, as fat
caterpillars crawled like larval angels
from Krubsack's mouth, I flew to Jesus,
cradled myself in his arms and was
comforted by his breath, by
gasoline and cinnamon.

TABLEAU IN A LUTHERAN CHURCH

Paralyzed by sin
the young man
kneels in a pew, facing Jesus—pastel robes
trimmed in gold, golden hair, beard,
blue eyes, all of tinted plaster, above the altar.

Overwhelmed by blood
the young man
kisses the out-turned
pierced hands. He forgets the promises
he's made to be good,
frightened in his bed.

Ecstatic
the young man weeps,
spends kisses in that exotic holy place.
Christ's warm skin.

True love embraces kith and kin,
woman and man, man and woman.

FOUR

WHAT JOHN DILLINGER MEANT TO ME

The Wisconsin lodge
where Dillinger slept
with Evelyn Frechette
in a musty bedroom
hung with staghorns
is legend, has become
locale.

>   *Last week there were arbutus*
>   *this week violets,*
>   *and next there will be snow.*

Here was Robin Hood,
thirsting, despising law,
loner, who by miracle
knew and fled,
left Evelyn behind,
her and her friend.

>   *And snow follows snow.*
>   *Flickers drill the trunks*
>   *of evergreens for grubs*
>   *and nuts stored there by squirrels.*

>   *Bears lie fallow,*
>   *the paps of summer in their dreams.*
>   *Skunks garner oil, rub*
>   *their legs together to quiet the seeping.*

I did not see the pustules
on his jaw, the chipped tooth
the crooked finger, the fact
that he had clap. His hands
were beautiful. His breath
as fragrant as one of
Solomon's lovers.

And his picture
on my bedroom wall,

pasted to the corrugated box
smashed flat and nailed
to the two-by-fours to
keep out cold! How immaculate
his stance before his Flivver!
Felt hat back
on his head, shirt sleeves
rolled above the elbow,
trousers high on the waist,
a band, Hollywood style,
set with pearls to hold them
tight. His legs spread wide,
and, held even with his navel,
his Tommy gun. Again
the stance, a perfect V,
zodiac man.

What had gone wrong
at the forked bridge
outside the town? What
had transpired at
Sunday School? Was it
poverty? Despair?
The wheel at the fair?

The gingerbread man
rides the stream
on the slick nose of the fox,
Robin Hood romps in a costume,
Arthur in armor.

NIGHT VISITOR

Night sweat, hard breathing.
Agate moonlight shed through the window,
as the outlaw, white-throated, in a white
shirt with rolled sleeves
strokes the sleeping boy's shoulder.

He lifts the boy and holds him
sheetless, nude. The boy tastes Dillinger's
mouth, the fleshed inner lip, the tongue,
the zinc-taste of warm water.
"Take me!" the boy pleads.
The creaking is the roof's wind,
the bronze spittle of the home.

RADIO REPORT

Dillinger stopped for gas in Guttenberg, Iowa, with three other men, in a black car with metal shields fit to the tire rims, extending down over the tires, to ward off gun-shots.

The gas station owner locked himself in the women's rest-room. When he emerged he found money left by the gangsters to pay for gas and candybars.

In Ames, Iowa, the town police set up a roadblock at the bottom of Watermelon Hill. When Dillinger's car appeared, going fast, with gunbarrels protruding, the police scattered and hid in the cornfields. Dillinger crashed through and drove on.

SNOW IMAGE

I quarry his image from snow.
The radio says he has fled—
to Wisconsin or Illinois.

On the roof in the moonlight, feet tread.
A man in a silver sky
wears holsters of stars.

Blood drenches the clothes my mother dries.
Blood frosts her fresh baked cake.

Dillinger's hand covers my eyes.
"Sleep," he says. "Sleep."
His face is on my pillow.

DILLINGER IN WISCONSIN

1.

He drives north, 300 miles,
in his Hudson Terraplane.
"Leach, you fucker," he exclaims,
"I'll get you! Purvis, you scum,
kinky-haired Hoover's pretty boy.
Shove this up your ass!"
Then he misses Billie who is in jail.
They are already on his trail.

2.

J. Edgar Hoover flails the roadside
trees. The stench of an Illinois jail
on the night breeze. Shotgun barrels
protrude from white birch trees.
North of Oshkosh, fallow rolling fields.

Jiggling lights (a Model-A Ford)
speeding. Dillinger detours. The auto
passes. No guns, horns, or whistles.
He has survived, in these pristine woods.

3.

He looks at who he was, before he dies—
if he should die. That damn gross penis!
huge prepuce, stone. Even at fifteen
it wouldn't let him alone, clumped
between his legs, obscene, in his overalls
or gabardines: big head, bemused,
nestling over the tight balls.

In school he hated the sperm-stench
and smegma in his clothes,
the stale wool, the pulpy skin
between his toes. He kept
to the far corners of the school.
Baths were once a week, as a rule,
in a galvanized tub placed near

a kitchen stool. His dad
rubbed his back, or his sister Audrey
might, if her husband wasn't home that night,
off playing poker with the boys
or smooching at the picture show.

4.
He stops beside the road.
He climbs out, yawns and inhales
the piney air. The stony road
reflects moonlight in its ruts,
dark spruce and tamarack spires.
Blueberry swamp.
Two more hours to Little Bohemia.

He thinks of Billie in her bed.
He kisses her nipples.
He cradles her head, then
thinks of how she'd bled
when he first took her.
His loins are parched.
He rubs his glans with snow.
"Billie, Billie," he says.
His perineum burns.
Hot copper moves over his lips.
He strokes his groin, harder! harder!

THE WATCH-DOGS

Earl Wanatka, saloon-keeper
now owns Little Bohemia
a touch of old Bavaria
fifty miles from Rhinelander
fifteen from Eagle River.

Two watch-dogs are barking.

Nan Wanatka tells her sister
the true identities of the strangers:
the man with the dyed red hair and the mole
is Dillinger. The others are Baby Face Nelson,
Nelson's wife Helen, Homer Van Meter,
Tony and Jean Caroll, Marie Conforti
and her Boston bull puppy, Pat Reilly,
Pat Cherrington and Roy Hamilton.

The watch-dogs keep on barking.

Wanatka joins his guests
in a pistol match by the garage.
The gangsters are poor shots.
They play ball.
Dillinger sends Reilly to St. Paul
for money and ammunition.
Pat Cherrington goes too—
she needs a physician.

The watch-dogs keep on barking.

SONG

He has gunpowder on his breath.
There is brandy on his lips.
He's an asphodel, a hyacinth folded
in this loving night.
They'll never find him here.

BIRTHDAY PARTY

Wanatka drives his son to a birthday party.
He has to wait—
for Dillinger sends Van Meter to guarantee
that Wanatka doesn't talk.

Wanatka balks, knows he is in danger
but decides to write a friendly
U.S. attorney, in the Windy City.

Nan tucks his note in her corset,
waits to sneak it to the post office.
The dogs are barking.

She pulls the throttle.
The engine keeps dying.
Finally, she propels the car towards Mercer.

COW

I heard the radio news at ten.
Dillinger was in Wisconsin.
I led our cow to a new pasture.
She walked calmly on. I followed.

At the first creek I let her graze:
marshgrass, brown, seed-headed,
resembling flax. She stood in the
whirling stream. Frogs leapt when
she moved. Red-winged blackbirds
warbled in cattails. A breeze.

NIGHT ACCIDENT

1.
Dillinger, "Public Enemy No. 1,"
is a vicious killer. If you see him
grab the nearest phone, keep
your wife and kids at home,
load your derringers.

2.
At 2 a.m. a commotion in the road.
Banging metal. A car has overturned.
A stranger staggers to our door.
We've never seen him before.
We watch through the window,
pretend we're not home.
We have no telephone.

3.
I fail to comprehend my cowardice.
I rationalize, say the man with the car
was drunk. And I couldn't shoot a gun,
never could, although dad gave me one,
a 22. Big hunter! Killing bees by
shoving the barrel in on top of them
inside morning glories! A bang, a pop.
A pollen-bag on a leg. A drop of snot.

SATURDAY AT LITTLE BOHEMIA

Baby Face Nelson pursues Nan Wanatka.
She reaches her brother's farm.
Lloyd rides on with her to Mercer.

She buys candy, ostensibly
for the birthday party. Nelson glares
through the window. Candy
is Nan's alibi, logical, if she
has to tell it.

Lloyd mails the letter
at the railroad station.
Nan tells her story.
Voss says they'll be dead before
Monday. He'll drive to Rhinelander
and phone the FBI.

PURVIS

1.
"What if it all stops?" thinks Purvis,
rushing to the plane. He's still
knotting his tie, wears his third
fresh suit of the day. Silk underwear.
Damp, cold scrotum.

Such limits: his plane in the lead,
a second is following,
owned by the actress Ann Harding.
Eleven agents boarding.
No chartered lanes, auto maps only.
A sick pilot, bush-leaguer.
300 miles, a three-hour flight
to Rhinelander.

2.
His bullet-proof vest
presses on his chest,
holding him warm,
free of bodily harm.
God must be looking down,
thinks Purvis. Fame
conceals her curves
in a rose. Purvis
in the movies! Nubile creatures
on the zoom, in pink bedrooms.
Boys eating boys, girls
eating girls, men eating
girls and boys . . .
and Daddy J. Edgar, Mentor . . .
He must stop Dillinger:
Dead or Alive!

WAITING

A fear-leaf
brushes the hood of Reilly's Flivver.
He reverses, speeds off
with the money and ammunition.
Upstairs Dillinger paces.
Something's wrong.
He wants to run, before dawn.
He sees men at the window.
A shape in a uniform
crouches in a tree.
He goes to the bar to wait
for Reilly.

BURNING

Nothing is crystal here—
mica in stone, iron-veins,
gravel on a hill where
partridge fluff, absorbing heat.
A weasel.

Everything is sullied, fits
of breath, death, or so it seems.

THE RAID

1.
A wheel brake
on Purvis' plane fails.
The plane tips over.
Purvis takes orders
from Clegg, another
of Hoover's officers.

They commandeer a revved-up
Ford and other autos.
The plan: three bullet-proof vested men
will storm the lodge, and five men
will file left towards the lake.
Another five will veer right.
It's still too cold for boats,
too cold for swimming.

2.
The roads are in spring thaw.
Two cars break down.
Eight men ride double on running boards,
burdened with shells and rifles.
They cling to freezing chrome with bare
fingers. Two miles from the lodge,
headlights off—eerie swamp sounds,
sluffed branches, frozen pines
jab men's faces.

3.
Wanatka's watch-dogs bark.
They've barked so much
Dillinger keeps on playing cards.
The G-Men start running.
They've lost their cover!

Two bartenders ask
why the dogs are howling.
Three locals start for the door,
for home. Five men, then, about

to leave the premises.
What should a frightened G-Man do?
Shoot the first thing that moves!

4.
Purvis shouts "Halt!"
Bullets shatter the auto glass
A young CCC cook is shot,
a gas salesman is wounded.
Eugene Boisneau does not move.
He's dead. Shot through the head.

5.
The agents tangle in a barbed-wire fence,
stumble into a trench. The gangsters
jump out an upper window
to a pile of snow below
rush to the bank, to the lake, and escape.
Purvis keeps firing slugs
at the front door and at the front window.

EVERYWHERE, YET NOWHERE

1.
He escaped, remained as elusive as air.
He seemed to be everywhere, yet nowhere.

2.
"Well,
they had Dillinger
surrounded
and was
all ready to shoot him
when he came out,
but then
another bunch of folks
came out ahead,
so
they just shot them instead.
Dillinger
is going to acci-
dentally get with
some innocent by-
standers some time,
then
he will get shot."—Will Rogers

CODA

NOW

1.
The farms are ploughed under, bulldozed, erased.
The trees are gone. The creeks diverted. Grass
where the slops were thrown is still fire-green.
My parents are dead.

2.
My early friends are grown—each has danced
most of a life away. Shy lovers and forward ones

toss in their beds, among the sheets and gauze
of sleep churn towards decay.

Each of us makes a pitch, tosses coals
upon hard fires, hoping for a flash of gold.

I'll settle for less: the mothering woods, a wolf
at my feet, and Dillinger, on his way to my table
and my warm bed.

3.
I have not taken his picture from my shelf,
nor his poster from my wall.

I've had my own flames, breath to burn.
I believe the real Dillinger got away.

They shot the man without a mole, without a scar.
There was a stand-in at the Biograph Theater.

FATHER: AS RECOLLECTION OR THE DRUG DECIDES

1.
He is at the table again,
after his absence.

Where have you spent the day?
dumped the truckrubble?

He had driven off at noon,
wearing shopcap and overalls—
to the store, he said, before
he puked, for milk
to flush out poison
drawn in with smoke
from welding galvanized metal
earlier that morning.

What have you eaten?
with whom spoken, fornicated?
You have been drinking.
It tells as you glance up
from your plate full of
warmed-over meat.

It is late.
A nighthawk has swept
its wings past, and the water
in the lake is chalk and silver.

On the cold stove
sit pots and pans
petals without arrangement
holding no milk

which you did not buy
which you will not touch
but which you will note
and remark upon

as mold encroaches

forms olive scum, foam
on clabbered ponds.

Once more
you have proved yourself a man.

2.
And he will wail.
His face will stream
with revilings. Self-
denigrations will clog
his nose, as he clambers out,
once again, out
of the smashed crib
of his childhood,
wailing for his mother

earth-struggler,
mechanic, lumberjack
tearing himself down
stripped into glass
balsawood, ravished
machine

mother dead
in an ironposted bed
belly rupture
and measles
and ratted hair
the sweat on her face
salt

and no consolation   none
none anywhere
no one
to scrape his pants
make meals—
his dad off
scavenging coal
from a decrepit mine
to hawk in town,
confront the whores.

3.
There is a price
a price to pay

which I share, share
as I spill these words
in a tongue
you never mastered, heard

as lice clamber, itch
in memory's dank black
pubic beard.

your evasions scald,
your submissions
passion and anguish
rancid self-equations
burn and freeze me.

I draw in my shoulders
press on this pen
caress the breath
slinking between
the syllables

correct that breath
shift, redirect it
grow bolder, long finally
for the stranger
to cross the doorsill
knife bared, scimitar:

one of
Rimbaud's indians, or Dillinger
intent upon setting our boats
moored as they have been
(the slaughtered haulers)
as they've seemed to be
with silken threads
adrift.

MOTHER

The resuscitation team had little time
for decency: his mother lay on the floor
with her nightie hiked around her neck.
The team seemed indifferent to the exposure:
the shanks, the little body like a worm
in a nutshell, the sagging breasts.

He grabbed an afghan from the couch, one
full of strong flower-colors, and covered
her parts.

The team kept thumping on her chest.
They clamped an oxygen cup over her mouth.
Nothing helped, as she sunk deeper
into the floor, through the cement slab,
lower than the potatoes.

ON NOT ATTENDING MY FATHER'S FUNERAL

1.
The land was rock and sand,
the growing season short,
the acreage minute.
We hoed potatoes, watched
corn grow, cultivated turnips
for the hogs to eat.
Dad was always there.

He barely wrote. He
almost never read. His
language, though, fed similes
and metaphors. He taught himself
to play six instruments. He could fix
anybody's car. He swung
farm implements as if
the earth loved his assault,
even when he was fatigued
he laughed. He often sang.
I could not bear
his absences at work.

He built a house
of timbers he himself had cut
and hewn. As we grew
he added other rooms,
modified the roof hip-style,
and piled rock, stoneboated
from the field, to build
a basement. He shot deer,
rabbit, quail. He caught fish
through the ice. His labors
were in pleasing us. We rode
to town with him in a model-A
sedan he'd converted to a truck.

He breathed in fumes
welding steel in shipyards
and drank to counteract the smoke.

He never saw a doctor, lived
on beer. Later, he bought
a welding shop, inhaled nore
fumes, cast the right seams
but never charged enough.
He reviled himself,
lamenting his dead brothers
and sisters, hungered for his mother.
He became one of us.
He stopped singing, spent hours
before the television set.

He built a second house
of cinder blocks. He never
finished it. Studs and two-by-fours
left bare, a primer coat of paint,
an unsmoothed concrete floor.
He was always cold.
His cars ran, but now never
with that earlier precision.
He was indifferent
to his gift of touch.

A bone prodded him.
He grew thin.
A cancer was removed. He walked
needing a stick, huddled
in a soiled overcoat.

2.
The town dump in mist and fog.
Girls brought a dog
for him to shoot. He placed the rifle
to its skull, pulled the trigger,
missed. He fell,
scrambled on the ground
in leafless brush, was dead.

3.
I won't see him dead!
A maudlin gathering of tears
over broken hands and arms

beat into shape
lifecolored by a cosmetologist!

Speak! dad. Sing!
Your visits in my dreams remain
benign!

The flesh I grasp—my own
my sons', my lover's—
is your continuing life.
My fantasies are yours, as is
my strength. I find
the animals you shot
huddled before me on the path.
I stroke their fur.
I see your houses, crops. Your
accordion and mandolin waltz past
me. Your metaphors dance and craze
my mind.

BURIAL

While the grave-digger
dug his mother's grave
squirrels romped beneath an oak tree.

The old digger cut quilt-exact
squares of turf and piled them
on a tarmac. His shovel
had a square end and easily cut through
the sand and roots.

His mother would lie beside his dad,
her concrete box containing her blue
coffin touching his gray concrete box
containing his brown coffin.

He had the digger pause while he stroked
his dad's box: dead twelve years—bones,
shredded clothes, and little black beads
for his eyes. The sand was carrot-red.
Would their juices, in the sense of mush,
blend through into some neutral space?

His mother preferred no coffins or cement—
just her corpse arranged feet down, head up,
in the sand. He had touched her hands
and kissed her forehead and knew
how iced-over death is.

Spiney carrot tops struck him in the face,
hard across the mouth.

ALSO AVAILABLE FROM THE SEA HORSE PRESS

THE BUTCH MANUAL by Clark Henley

Not everyone was born Butch, but now everyone can become masculine beyond their wildest dreams—that is if you can stop laughing long enough. Henley's hilarious social satire is illustrated with amusing photographs.

ISBN-0-933322-11-9 $6.95 Paper

DREAMLOVERS by Pete Fisher

Charting one man's search to turn fantasy into reality—despite a lover, a career, and uncomprehending friends. *Dreamlovers* is Pete Fisher's wildest, sexiest and most involving book.

ISBN-0-933322-07-0 $8.95 Paper

AN ASIAN MINOR: The True Story of Ganymede
by Felice Picano

What happens when a thirteen year old boy discovers he is the most beautiful mortal ever born? The hero of this retelling of the Greek myth has been compared to Huck Finn and Molly Bolt. 12 B & W illustrations by David Martin.

ISBN-0-933322-06-2 $6.95 Paper $12.95 Hardcover

A TRUE LIKENESS: Lesbian & Gay Writing Today

33 Writers: Fiction, poetry and short drama by Andrew Holleran, Edmund White, Judy Grahn, Emily Sisley, George Whitmore, Jane Rule, etc.

ISBN-0-933322-04-6 $9.95 Paper

TWO PLAYS BY DORIC WILSON: *A Perfect Relationship* and *The West Street Gang*

Productions of these funny, slick, wise plays across the country have made Doric Wilson one of the best known gay playwrights and social critics.

ISBN-0-933322-01-1 $5.95 Paper

IDOLS: Poems by Dennis Cooper

Trenchant, erotic and controversial poems by one of the most remarkable young gay poets in years.

ISBN-0-933322-02-X $4.95 Paper

THE DEFORMITY LOVER and Other Poems by Felice Picano

This first book of poems by the novelist became an instant classic upon publication. Fourth printing.

ISBN-0-933322-00-3 $3.95 Paper

Available at Price + $1.00 shipping from
THE SEA HORSE PRESS
307 West 11th St., N.Y.C. 10014